ISBN 9781088973110

Dedicated to my three extraordinary stepchildren:

Brooklynn, Jacob and Nathan.

After my big brother Hurley had completed his mission and went to heaven, I was sad.

I was lonely.

I was confused.

Ever since I was a tiny puppy, I had been with Hurley. He had shown me how to be a good dog. He had taken care of me and been my best friend.

Mom and Dad were heartbroken, and they were also concerned for me. I wasn't myself, and neither was anyone else in our house.

Mom and Dad talked and talked, and they knew
what they needed to do; for them, for my
brothers, but mostly for me.

One day, a woman came to the door. I didn't know who she was, but my mom seemed to. She and my mom went to her car. I waited, wondering what was going on.

And then, I realized why this woman was here. They were walking back to the house...with a puppy!

Oh no! Was I being replaced?

I wasn't.

Mom and Dad were giving me a new brother. They named him Pugsley, so his name would go with mine (two characters on a funny TV show).

I found out that he came from a breeder. The people who were in charge only sold "perfect" dogs, and Pugsley had a physical flaw. They decided he wasn't worth anything.

I think Pugsley was too young to understand.

He was lucky.

It wasn't long before my smile came back!

How could I not smile when my new best buddy
had a heart on his nose?!

I loved my new brother!

We did everything together, and for once I got to be a big sister.

(That didn't last long, though).

I missed Hurley every day, but I knew Pugsley
needed us.

And we needed him.

At first, I could tell that my mom felt a little guilty about adopting a new dog, but that didn't last long.

She could see how joyful I was again and how many smiles Pugsley brought our family, including her!

Mom knew that she and Dad had done the right thing.

"It's almost like Hurley sent Pugsley to us, isn't it?"
Mom said. "Hurley knew we'd need someone to
make us smile and laugh again."

"Hurley did send him, I'm sure of it!" I replied.

People started to tell Mom that they'd been inspired by our story to adopt a new pet after losing one that they'd loved dearly.

Our whole family knew that we were spreading a
good message: that it's okay to love again after
loss!

All thanks to Pugsley, The Heart-Nosed Healer.

There are far too many dogs and cats out there who need a loving home. If we close our hearts and our doors, who will help them?

They need us.

And we need them.

Wednesday and Jack

Wednesday and Chewy

New brother Pugsley arrives!

Pugsley gets to know the family

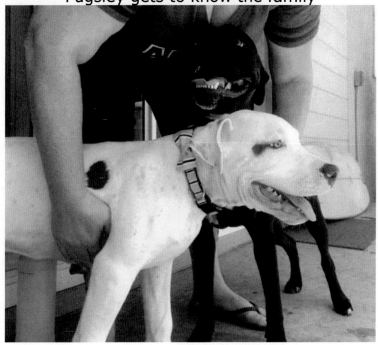

Pugsley makes himself at home

Pugsley fitting right in!

Pugsley outgrows Wednesday

Brother love

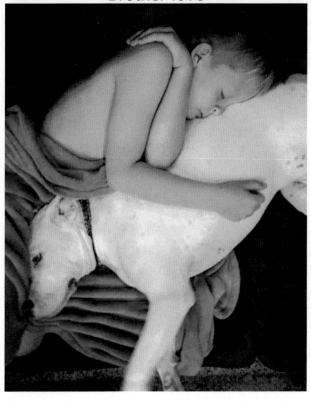

Happy family!

ABOUT THE AUTHOR

Di is an actress and writer who lives in Southern California with her husband, stepchildren and menagerie of pets. If you share her love of pit bulls and kitties and animals in general, follow her on social media for non-stop laughs and entertainment.
@aTaleOf2Pitties

11596532R00021

Made in the USA
Monee, IL
13 September 2019